Miss Plastique

ALSO BY LYNN LEVIN

POETRY
Fair Creatures of an Hour 2009
Imaginarium 2005
A Few Questions about Paradise 2000

TRANSLATION
The Forest: Poems by Besnik Mustafaj 2000 (chapbook)

NONFICTION
Poems for the Writing: Prompts for Poets 2013
(with Valerie Fox)

MISS PLASTIQUE

POEMS

LYNN LEVIN

Ragged Sky Press
Princeton, New Jersey

Published by Ragged Sky Press
P.O. Box 312, Annandale, NJ 08801
www.raggedsky.com

Library of Congress Control Number: 2012954086

ISBN: 978-1-933974-12-5

Cover and book design: Bill Donnelly/WT Design
Photograph of author: Beverly Collins-Roberts

Cover Art: *Jett,* one of The Dynamite Girls by Integrity Toys.
Copyright © by Integrity Toys. Used by permission.
Photograph of *Jett:* Christina Goodison

Printed in the United States of America

First Edition

This book is for all the teachers
who had faith in me,
starting with Mrs. Marian Hay
in the ninth grade.

CONTENTS

IV

I

SOME FIRST THOUGHTS

Apple of my eye.
Attic with a window.
Little mountain, little alp
before the Big Bang, you! Nothing anterior.
Of marks in school, there is none better
than your happy little tent.
Without you no kid could wail for his ma
no doctor examine a sore throat.
Take away A—
the human heart heaves hermetic.
Aleph. Alpha. A. Alif.
In most *abecedarios*
you are the first letter. And it is good
to begin in accord
to agree on anything
however simple and small.
After that, when paths diverge
and endings or the visions of endings differ…
Well, that is not the business of A.

Miss Plastique

Because it should be handled
with care and can explode
at any moment, it is like me.
Picture a gob of it molded
into the Three Graces—
Shock, Orgasm, and Wrath.

Watching *The Man from U.N.C.L.E.*
I thrilled to see Illya Kuryakin
pack plastique into a keyhole
then coolly turn as it blew
open a door. Imagine!
Something that looks like dough

can kill you. I love the stuff
with a self-love
I never knew I had.
More than my stiletto
heels, Garbo hat, or lipsticks.
I want to wrap some up like bubble gum
and give it to my enemy:
Here. Take me into your mouth. Taste me.

FAUX KING IN THE PARKING LOT

It was in the parking lot
at the Samba Club
between sets at the Huxley wedding

and he was an Elvis impersonator.
We'd eyed each other during "Love Me Tender,"
through his heavy lashes he nodded me over.

Ah, to be taken without being adored.
Though to be adored without being taken
is also a wonder.

Those silver studs on his white suit.
The Brylcreem (I didn't know
they still made it)

left oil stains, dammit, on my nice
linen skirt. Techno boinked from a passing car
and we pumped to it.

He said his wife didn't
understand him. "I never sleep with happily
married men," I told him.

Curling his lip, the faux king shot
"Then you ought to sleep
with your husband."

I should have slapped him.
But his thighs were hot
and the side of the car was cold.

ACTION HERO

Racks of blouses. Bangles of cherry, lime, banana plastic.
Jo Beth started buying that junk as soon as she could spend
her babysitting money or the cash her father
handed her after he'd surprise her in the shower. "Doesn't that beat
all?" she'd say. "He'd turn off the hot water. I'd yell
bloody murder. I was twenty-two then." What a monster

Tim thought. As a boy Tim loved models of monsters—
the Swamp Thing, Frankenstein, dozens of other scary plastic
creatures he glued together alone in his room. His dad yelled,
"Why can't you play baseball like the other boys?" Tim hated to spend
time with his dad. Some nights Pop would wake the boy and beat
him for poor grades or bad reports from the bus driver. His father

couldn't stand failure. Hearing he was going to be a father,
Tim couldn't wait to tie the knot with Jo Beth. "She's not a monster,"
Tim told his folks, though she'd done hard time for beating
an infant she babysat. Now she buys their son Matt plastic
action figures like The Incredible Hulk. She loves to spend
so Matt gets a new toy each day. That shopping makes Tim yell

at her. He'll curse her sometimes. Both of them yell
so loud that neighbors often call the cops. "You're a lousy father!"
Jo Beth screams, "just like your fucking pop." Then she'll spend
rent money on more X-Men, later crying that she has a monster
migraine and must be rushed to the ER. She has dozens of plastic
hospital bracelets. Between gut pains and headaches, she must be at

a clinic several times a week. At this point she hasn't beaten
Matt, but she sleeps with him naked. He's tired at pre-K and yells
at the other kids. The teacher sends home notes. With her plastic,
Jo Beth bought Matt a Dracula. Through the son comes the father
and through the father the son. So, too, the daughter. A monster
can be slain by a hero, but Tim and Jo Beth have to spend

a lifetime trying to appease demons, and their strength is spent
paying daily tribute. Still, brutal history can change its heartbeat.
Tim and Matt laugh together reading tales of silly monsters.
Yet when Tim speaks of divorce, Jo Beth weeps and yells,
"I love you! Don't leave me!" He sighs and gets no farther
than the front door, walks back through the hordes of plastic.

Matt enjoys spending days with his dad, who doesn't yell
that much at him. Tim has the heartbeat of a model father.
He hopes monsters can change. He wants nature to be plastic.

IDYLLS OF MAYFIELD

America during the days of *Leave It to Beaver*
was so gentle: even the war was a Cold War. Wally
never worried about finding himself, and Ward
knew he was blessed with well-adjusted kids and beautiful June
who always looked up to him. Oh orderly suburbs! Oh Mayfield!
whose major troubles came from the mind of Eddie Haskell

who wouldn't quit giving Beav the business. Eddie Haskell
who got Wally to break curfew and urged Beaver
to sign up for the modeling agency. Remember Mayfield's
soup-bowl billboard? Beaver scaled it the night of Wally's
teen party and got stuck in the bowl. I bet June
was hysterical. "Next time don't take foolish dares," counseled Ward

who parented per Spock, spared the rod. And Ward
never forgot that he'd been young once. Eddie Haskell
wasn't as lucky in the dad department, but did he flatter June,
"You look lovely today, Mrs. Cleaver!" Sure Beaver
understood that Eddie was two-faced, but he was Wally's
best friend. I never figured out why in all of Mayfield

Wally couldn't find a better best friend. Anyhow, life after Mayfield
wasn't easy for Ken Osmond. He could only look forward
to smarmy-guy roles and finally became a cop with the LAPD. Was Wally
scratching his head about that, thinking how ironic that Eddie Haskell
was making other people follow the rules? After *Beaver*
Jerry Mathers earned a BA in philosophy and a bundle in real estate. June

would have been proud. And Eddie was right. June
was a vision in shirtwaists and pearls, always dressed to go out in Mayfield
though she never went anywhere. Staying home for Wally and Beaver
seemed to fulfill her. She had that kind of grace and in Ward
a decent guy who managed a smile whenever Eddie Haskell
came to the door. Yet how could that boy not envy Wally?

Clean-cut, smart, well liked, a letterman in sports, Wally
was ripe for Eddie's corruption and certainly June
kept an eye out, maybe pitied him too, for I suspect Eddie Haskell
felt bad about himself the way the less loved, less talented may feel
bad about themselves. The Cleavers found fate kinder. They had Ward
who listened and fixed what he could fix so that Beaver

and Wally could have a happy childhood in Mayfield.
Sometimes I wished my parents were like June and Ward,
but I always laughed when Eddie Haskell messed with Beaver.

II

BEING ME

Being me is a kind of neurosis
but sometimes I have fun between crises.
As a kid, I once identified a copperhead

by looking it straight in the eye.
It really did have vertical pupils
like a cat's. I yelled *poisonous!*
and the other girls and boys ran off.

In those days, I wasn't very nearsighted
but I was very fond of cats.
Remembering my childhood

is like putting my hand down
the garbage disposal
and hoping no one will turn it on.

When I wasn't
spreading butterflies, I played
undertaker with my cousins:

first makeup, then the footlocker.
Live burial, I found, was not for me.
Instead of birding, now I watch Navy jets.

The F16s always fly in pairs
as if they were scared or mating.
Will Mitchell ever call?

It's been ten years…
I didn't like being lost in the middle
of the night on a Jersey highway.

On my way to the bed and breakfast
I took every wrong exit. I thought
I was going to have to start

a completely new life.
I have an excellent homing device
for error. It's only natural—

dark energy controls most of the world
and pulls me I-don't-know-where
but not to dinner with Danny and Marge.

I wish I could remember your name
the way I remember every mean thing
anyone's ever said to me.

Have you played *Police Chase?*
The one with the most felonies and damage
wins. When my client ordered

a fourth redirect of my direct-mail kit
for *The Anti-Stress Handbook,*
I said *fuck you!* and quit the project.

Then I had the whole afternoon
to weed my garden.

THE FOUNDATIONS OF POETRY

"I'd like all the boys to step out of the classroom,"
commanded Mrs. Hay whose mouth looked like a small crescent
    of radish.
How she could enunciate or open wide enough
to eat corn on the cob was beyond me.
Instead of discussing Shakespeare's sonnets that day
she gave us ninth-grade girls a lecture

about our miniskirts and what she thought was
our protruding underwear.
"Some of you have no sense of shame.
Just the other day I saw a girl tugging at her girdle.
You should never wear clothes
that leave those things exposed."

Beneath awnings of mascara, we rolled our eyes.
It was the spring that slit-paneled dresses
with matching shorts were the rage, and I was concerned
that, being older, she took the shorts for girdles.
Thank God that by tenth grade they'd invented
pantyhose. No more binding foundations
that strangled the thigh, making the pudge
bulge just over the elastic.
Finally we were free
from garter belts—all those tabs and hooks
in which we had to catch
the slippery tops of our stockings.
When we wore knits, always those telltale bumps from the tabs.
Really, it was so embarrassing to be a woman.

"What the hell's that?" pruded my student
when years later I showed my class an old garter belt.
Like Mrs. Hay, not comprehending
the mysteries of female fashion
he assumed that we went to junior high school
bottomless and crotchless,
all of us nasty girls beneath our clothes.

"You should expose
your thoughts and feelings
when you write poems," taught Mrs. Hay.
"In verse, a little thigh is fine
and you may dream your truth into your lines.
Only do not lie to yourself."

By now Mrs. Hay's at least 108,
and I still think of her counsel,
still wonder what made her wear
half-inch bangs and crazy pin curls plastered
around her large rectangular head.
I see her now as Juno,
statue-gray and old school,
one of the finest teachers I ever had.

DIPPITY-DO

I hated my hair and wished it were straight
so that I could wear it
in a swing or the London Look.
I wanted my hair to be smooth
so the popular girls
would talk to me at school.
Also wished my father
didn't get mad almost every night.
Once he knocked
all the rollers from my head.
The few bobby pins left
dangled like snot
from the wild curls I'd finally caught
with just enough Dippity-do.
I think that set took me an hour.
After that, I let my hair go free.
The straight kids thought I was a head.
You look like Janis Joplin, the hippies said.
And, hey, that was good enough for me.

EDDIE PRATT AS HIMSELF

WARMINSTER, PA 1991

After a photograph by David Graham

Oh imp!
Eddie, your lips Cherries in the Snow
your bustier and panties
redder than salvia, than the dream of ketchup
in a stark-raving white diner.
Once the world was a school
where you had to write:
I will act like a man
100 times on the blackboard.
Now your fishnets croon
and your eyes keen:
I don't want to be loved.
I want to be exposed.

MISS NEW YORK PRINCESS

Perfect as plastic with camera smiles,
updo'ed hair, look-at-me eyes,
these girls, the four-to-sixes,

tiniest princesses, pageant-walk the stage
in their ice cream-colored gowns.
Fidgeting in hotel chairs, the moms—

ex-cheerleaders, ex-queens of proms,
some who, never seen as lovely,
passed loveliness on to their daughters.

Golden trophies rise like little skyscrapers
on a table by the stage: one for best in playwear,
best thank-you note, best resume.

After Bink, the tux'd emcee, gives
each chosen child her prize, "My Girl"
lullabies through the gravid air.

A hush descends. He names and crowns
Miss New York Princess, who beams
as clouds of bubbles champagne down.

Then through the ballroom doors one mom,
a tulle bouquet sobbing in her arms,
runs (she can't run fast enough)
from this court of beauty and charm.

HITCHHIKER

Because I would not stop for him,
    he sprinted after me
as I pulled to a red light.
    I could have chosen charity
but I didn't. Big-eyed and hopeful, he
    hooked my gaze like a bass, then flashed a cardboard sign:
Hungry. Will work for food.
    and an alligator smile from somewhere in his hoodie.
Don't be stupid, I told myself,
    locked the doors, sweated out the light,
spied in the side-view mirror the hard-boiled eggs of his eyes
    and, not his thumb, but his middle finger.
A shame these days that so many kidnappers and murderers

    have given hitchhikers a bad name
for I myself had been a hitchhiker
    when carless in Texas and careless, too
lazy to shoe leather the mile to the bus stop
    or late for work, I thumbed rides.
When I was lucky, good old boys with honest mud on their jeans
    would pick me up in their beat-up chariots,
eight-tracks playing Willie Nelson or Waylon Jennings.
    Truth was, most folks in cars ignored me
but one April morning when the bluebonnets
    Maybellined the roadsides,
a man pulled over in a black Gran Torino

    and I didn't even have my thumb out.
Skullish face, dead tooth, watery eyes
    this was Tom Wise, who said he was a social worker
downtown and took me all the way
    to the bank where I worked—
and maybe he wondered why a gal with a proper job

was accepting rides from strangers
but he didn't ask.

Next day he wore a green silk tie
and reeked of Aramis: a real lady-killer.

Still, I liked not having to take the bus.
So I got in,

but this time he wanted my phone number.
"Don't worry. I just want to give you a buzz,"

he simpered around his brown incisor.
"I won't bite you…unless that's your thing."

I was smart, gave him a fake number.
Later, in case I'd have to wring

this sorry mess out to the cops,
I tried to hunt him down in the phone book

but found no Tom Wise or Wyse or even Weiss.
 Then I got the idea that he was a pimp.

Something about the social work and the downtown thing.

Next day Tom pulled over. I waved "no thanks."

Only he stayed parked on the shoulder.
But I wasn't dumb, I crossed

to the other side. He swung a U-ey. I doubled back,
and it went on like that a few times

until, foiled, he bared his torqued tooth,
skewered the air with his bony, middle-aged, middle finger.

This made the world a huge drive-in movie theater
and the two of us stars in its fright show.

Afterward, I feared I'd see Tom Wise
pulling up behind me, idling at a light.

Was spared that, but I remember
the pine-tree air freshener dangling from his dash,

the bluebonnets blooming outside his safety glass.

III

The House on Blackberry Lane

This is the house on Blackberry Lane.

This is the husband who kindled a fire
in the house on Blackberry Lane.

This is the log, fat as a cask,
trundled in by the husband to stoke the fire he kindled
in the house on Blackberry Lane.

This is the wife who asked the husband
not to add the log, fat as a cask, because it could roll
from the fireplace and burn down
the house on Blackberry Lane.

This is the irk
that stirred in the husband
asked by the wife, fearful of flames,
not to add the log, fat as a cask,
to the fire he built
in the house on Blackberry Lane.

This is the carpet fire
sparked by the log that rolled from the hearth
as feared by the wife
who asked the husband
not to add the log, fat as a cask,
to the fire he built
in the house on Blackberry Lane.

This is the haste of the wife who rushed to the window
to clear the smoke that fumed from the fire
ignoring the husband who yelled, "Don't open that window!"
because she guessed he was trying to deny
that the carpet was in flames
due to the log, fat as a cask, that rolled from the hearth
in the house on Blackberry Lane.

This is the window
that fell on the hand of the wife
causing a bloody mess
and squashing her wedding ring
because it was a faulty window
which the husband didn't fully explain
because he was busy heaving the log, fat as a cask,
back into the fireplace and stamping out the carpet fire
in the house on Blackberry Lane.

These are the tin snips
in the hand of the husband who said, "This is rich.
I gave you that ring, and now I'll remove it."
Still he freed from its golden vise
the throbbing finger of the wife,
who rushed to the window to clear the smoke
fumed by the flames, sparked by the log, fat as a cask,
that rolled from the hearth
in the house on Blackberry Lane.

This is the new ring
bought by the husband who pledged fresh devotion
to the same old wife who managed to love him.
And this is the new gray Berber
in the house on Blackberry Lane.
Now may further talk be banned
of the tin snips that freed
the window that slammed
the smoke that fumed, the carpet in flames
and as for the log, fat as a cask,
let nothing more be said of that.

INSOMNIAC ROMANCE

We hate to hate each other but we do—
then feeling bad because of that we lay us
next to next in bed, two statues on a tomb.
We want to crash to sleep but can't
reliving meannesses and fights that flicker past
as dumb shows in the cemetery light.
But leave you? I do not think I could.
I like what carries on. I like the in-and-out
sound of your breath and your warm skin,
my steadfast partner, in the practice death.

VACATION

With binoculars I spy you on the links
late August breeze upon your midlife brow.
A snack-cart girl in shorts comes by to sell
you beer, to light your Davidoff cigar.
I should be at the spa. Instead I dolphin watch
on the kelp-strewn beach where thirsty surf
sucks rocks and invisible horses clop
with their invisible burdens of onions. Sun
stuck like a burner on high, crab pinching the air.
It's like a vision from *The Time Machine*. But no:
this is the good life. You're on the resort
course with the guys aiming for birdies and pars
not trying to pick up women in the hot
tub or the hotel bar. I couldn't be happier.

YES NO MAYBE

Do you love me? she asks. He says *yes*
to comfort her, but he doesn't know
if he's being honest. The habit of caring may be

what binds them now, and in this world maybe
that's not a bad routine. Though yes-
terday their house swarmed with the old arrows. There's no

Magic 8-Ball for them, a seer to declare: no
you should not give up. There may be
hope for you yet. Or absolutely yes,

yes, one of you should find a new address. No more
procrastination. Or maybe wait: do nothing in haste.

TO A RIVAL

Some say the world is big enough for all of us
but I think you take up too much space
in the book review section.
I hate the way you
in the destructive element immerse
your meters and swift procession of tropes,
your book prize, your Japanese garden.
Here's the worst—
every time I see you with him
I feel the same hot surge I felt
when I realized I'd left the copper kettle on high,
all the water boiled out,
and I almost burned down my house.
Thank God your nose looks like a can opener
or I'd have another reason to detest
your ingenious blend of the sentimental and sarcastic.
But if you phoned and said
Let's go out to lunch
I think, R., we could be friends.

Hotel Paradox

If I slept, I dreamed I stayed awake
all night. If I ate, I spooned the soup
of hunger. If I took a bath, I came out
covered with dust and sweat. The more jackets
I wore, the colder I felt. I tried

to rest though the springs of the bed attacked.
Like a good guest I complimented the cook
on his miserable chowder. I let my rival
wash my back, and I washed hers
as envy warmed us with its little stove.

Oh, to rise from my nervousness like a carp
from a dark pool or eat half portions when I crave
the whole poison. What soap can wash away
my foolishness or deep years wake me?

A Piece of Silk

You with that gold ring in your nose
you sleeping in his tent each night
with all those pillows
you at his side when he visits kings
you whose hands are fine enough
to bake bread for angels
just remember I'm the one he runs to
when he fears death.
He grows hard just being near me.

Do you think we've stopped seeing each other?
Under the pomegranate tree he often visits me.
Sometimes we even speak of making a little brother
for our Ishmael.
He gave me gifts the other day—
some eye paint and a piece of silk
so fluid that if I were in the desert and thirsty
I could drink it.

Oh! Do not send me away!

I know that I'm the concubine and you're the wife.
But, sister, listen.
It's not you or I.
What he really loves is that Voice.
That Voice
with its wings, its claws.
He's so afraid that it will leave him.

THE NOTEBOOK

An adaptation of Gaspara Stampa's sonnet CXXXII

I ask for Love's attention through my tears—
Love who can scarcely turn his head my way
though I ask a thousand times a day.
The reason? Those other lips about his ears.
His silence rips my heart, it tears
my dress, the pages of my books. Pray
how can this be? I gave my heart and soul away
to him. There's nothing left in me. He cares
little for my grief. I feel my blood run
like an icy stream of envy, dread.
He was my life's great joy and reason.
Now I die in love. I live in pain. In bed
I have a notebook and a quill. Let him shun
me. On these sheets he's mine, though I am dead.

THE GRIP

It makes no sense to break with you and sigh
repeat with the rain its dull and penitent part.
For us the normal rules do not apply.

We are the best of bed friends. Why
pass up pleasure when life's dreary and short?
It makes no sense to break with you and sigh.

In musty day-rate rooms we lie
and swoon the animal swoon. Sweetheart
we're lovers! The normal rules do not apply

to us. Besides, your guilt's a bore, and I
am slimmer, younger, prettier, a good sport
about nights and weekends. Break with you and sigh?

Resign with selfless honor? As long as you tie
me to the bedpost, help with rent, I'll feel smart
and happy. Extraordinary rules apply

to girls like me. Though some nights I cry
with envy and curse your greedy heart.
It might make sense to break with you and sigh—
or break with me if normal rules apply.

THE LANGUAGE OF WILDFLOWERS

Teasel, primrose, touch-me-not.
Frostweed, snow-on-the-mountain.
Goat's beard, mandrake, cockspur thorn.
Honeysuckle, kisses, foxglove, beard-tongue.
Nightshade, shooting stars.
Jack-in-the-pulpit.
Loosestrife, hell vine, bittercress, rue.
Compass plant, heal-all, fever-few.
Four-o'clock.
Forget-me-not.

PEOPLE CAN GET USED TO JUST ABOUT ANYTHING

If, like him, you ate rats in the sideshow
you'd make it look easy, too, with white bread
and years of practice. Truth is, the first time
you swallowed a rat, you wished you were dead.

It gagged you on the way down your throat
dug through your sleep, backstroked in your gut
ate and shit where it ate. You swore you'd never
gulp another rat and suffer, but

you're weak. Anyway, the second time you knew
how to protect your gullet from its claws
and learned to love its scamper simply because
it was familiar, came to recognize that pause

before it bites as a chance to give it cheddar.
Skrik! it says in thanks. You feel better.

To a Lamprey

Lord of the soft lash
sharp straw
you scar
so many fish
with your kisses
root and drink
the perch down
to the white shame
of its bones.
Whose mouth wants you
that much
would take everything
out of you
if only you'd let it?
You merely dream
of the twining and untwining
the untwining and twining
then waking up
untouched
hate yourself in the morning.
How much I am like you, vampire—
neither of us
knows pleasure
until we are
half self, half other
or no self at all.
Small wonder
that we hate daylight
and the sight of ourselves
in mirrors.
Perhaps a psychiatrist
would help us

accept ourselves
or change
into a bridge
an open window
a door ajar.
This is the way out
I would sing
as I abandoned
my thirst and my hunger.

PLEASE UNDERSTAND

I love to say your name, it's like candy
in my mouth. I love to say your name,
it's like saltwater taffy.
When I steal a look at your eyes
it's like I'm shoplifting in a jewelry store,
and my heart's arrested
when you catch me.
What an old fool I am.
You are my student, raw and strange,
a genius monster with long dark hair,
a baseball cap, and flip-flop sandals.
Though it burns my lips like chili lipstick
and licks with vodka flame
bitter, hot and arctic,
I love to say your name.
Should our two storms combine
we'd be like his and hurricanes, we'd plow
acres of disaster and after would arrive
a peculiar kind of fame, a dog
that through the ruins yaps and sniffs
and wags its tail excited by the shame.
I have nightmares of us
on the quad. Outside of class
what would we talk about—
your mom and dad, your iPod?
And suppose you had a special girl?
How terrible for me to learn
you were not miserable.
Still, it's a gift to know impossible love.
Think of Petrarch and how he pined for Laura.
I, too, sing of amorous suffering.
But because I sing of you
it's not for nothing.

THIS LIFE

Love pulled me out of myself, the way a cook eviscerates a chicken.
Cut me open and you will find his fingers.

&

Your mouth is a honeyed shape of air.
Hand me a knife. I will slice an apple to dip in it.

&

You comb my hair desiring more tangles.
Then we stand in the wind together and hold hands.

&

Sometimes I submit to the truth
hoping it is merciful.

&

When a lover leaves you
you say, *Thank you*

then wipe your mouth with the next day's napkin
erase help and sleep from the blackboard.

&

The old corrupter rises again to defend himself
before the young and the living.

&

In ruins the sky will pose with clouds
and a tree in the rose window.

&

The body of one should depart for the body of the other
but some ghosts would like to stop at walls.

&

For a few months I turned away from the mirror.
Now I cannot look back.

IV

EVE AND LILITH BACK AT THE GARDEN

Eve and Lilith peered through
the padlocked gates of the garden,
now a restricted community.

Eve glared at Lilith,
"You told me it was easier to beg
forgiveness than ask permission. Now look."

"That's what *I* always do," Lilith replied,
aware that under the circumstances
she sounded pretty lame.

"Plus," said Eve, "I think I'm pregnant."
"I told you to use protection," said Lilith.
"But Adam promised..." Lilith rolled her eyes.

"Him and his teaspoon of joy," said Eve.
A fault line threatened her brow.
"Girlfriend," counseled Lilith,

"either change your life or accept your life
but don't go around mad.
Let that anger go," said Lilith. "Just let it go."

Eve hated it when her friend got preachy.
Anyhow when it came to holding onto anger
Eve was an Olympian, a gold medalist.

She clung to a grudge
like a shipwrecked sailor to a scrap of wood.
It had something to do

with her excellent memory.
As Eve sucked on the red lollipop of her hurt
the two women trudged back to Nod.

All of a sudden something dark
waved in the grass.
"Eek!" shrieked Lilith. "A snake!"

She high-stepped in panic.
Oh, woman-up, thought Eve
as she grabbed a Y-shaped stick,

immobilized the critter's head,
stared straight into its eyes.
The snake looked back at her with a *who me?* look.

"This one's harmless.
It's only a dumb animal," said Eve.
"Kill it! Kill it!" pleaded Lilith.

"Sorry," said her friend. "No can do."
Eve let the snake go.
She just let it go.

EVE AND LILITH GO TO MACY'S

In the fitting room at Macy's
Eve shimmies into a pair of leopard-print leggings
then mocks a dance pose.
"OMG! You're hotter than a habanero in those pants,"
gasps Lilith. She slides her finger
down Eve's shapely hip
as though striking a match
then blows out her finger.

Eve can't believe how good that feels
through the cotton-polyester-spandex blend.
Lilith always went for men in a big way
but maybe the oversexed act
was overcompensation, a put-on.
Maybe Lilith is gay.
Maybe *I'm gay*, thinks Eve
wishing her friend would touch her again.

In the Macy's fitting room
with the triple-paneled mirror
the women's figures mingle and multiply.
Looking at one of her selves
Eve moves her right arm
but in the mirror it looks like her left arm.
She can't be sure which image
reflects the real Eve.

In the champagne of the moment
she turns to Lilith, the real one, the warm one
intending to bestow upon her
an air kiss of gratitude
at most a smooch on the cheek,

but Lilith catches Eve's mouth,
draws her to her other self.
Eve can't remember
when she's ever had a kiss like that.
Maybe she never has, never will again
so what is the point in stopping?

The women linger in each other's arms
as the hidden security camera
looks on with its mysterious eye.
And the women are okay with that.
They know that eye sees all things.
Sees all. Says nothing.

LILITH AT THE COSMETICS COUNTER

Lilith's face made a face at her
in the lighted mirror at the cosmetics counter.
Craggy, ravined, parched,
that thing above her neck looked like the Sinai Desert.
Yesterday militants high on toxic rumors
baby killer! man raper!
had run her out of town. Again.
She needed some ego first aid.
New address, new name, plastic surgery—
all that in good time.

"You look as one who has returned
from a long journey. This makeup will help,"
said the saleslady. She tilted her head
toward Lilith as if to say
we're all in this together
then tried to sign her up for a store credit card:
20% off all first-day purchases
including cosmetics!
The lady also happened to be
missing a front tooth.
Her false eyelashes were so thick
she gave everyone the hairy eyeball.

She began to fuss with her brushes
(probably not clean)
and pots of color
(no doubt contaminated by frequent double dipping).
Lilith was about to put herself
under the other woman's power
when she detected a whiff of sabotage
in the jasmine of her perfume.

Advice from an old lover tapped Lilith on the shoulder:
never buy makeup from someone
who's not as good looking as you.

Lilith glanced at the high-def mirror.
The wilderness of her face looked back at her
with weird familiarity. Haggard
is good enough for me, she decided,
thanked her saboteur and slid from the chair.
She knew her fate was a bitch
but it was *her* bitch.
And that was the beauty of it.

LILITH'S QUILT

Older, moonswept no more
Lilith saw bed as a place to sleep
but sleep abandoned her
like the millions of guys she'd had.
Every night she tossed and turned
with memories of her God-awful sex life—

the lovers who woke up terrified
dumped her out of the sack
mocked her desire.
Did a man ever live who could mix
with her body and soul?

To court slumber Lilith began to stitch
a quilt, a gift for her bed.
Each morning she gathered
scraps of colorful fabric
appliquéd scenes of the good life—
families at supper, workers at work,
weddings, births, kisses in the park.

By afternoon squares of human happiness spread
before her like the funnies in the newspaper.
Her scenes itched for a little disappointment.
But how much disappointment
did the good life allow—
a setback once a season,
a letdown once a week, once a day?

Lilith drove herself nuts with self-doubt.
Just before bed, she would take
a seam ripper to her beautiful squares
then collapse on her sheets.

Every morning, same story.
Lilith got up craving sleep like caffeine,
purple purses under her eyes.
She would gather her scraps
of colorful cloth and pat her bed.
"Old friend," she would say, "this time
I will finish the quilt
and then we will sleep like lambs."

TWELVE LIPS

1. Unmasking the clementine, I saw that its sweetness comprised twelve lips—
   at its center nothing but an inaudible whistling.

2. Heraclitus said, "Only change is changeless." My mother says, "People don't change."
   But Heraclitus was flexible, and my mother is stubborn.

3. If only I could gossip
   and not be the subject of it.

4. The soul cries out upon being recognized,
   then love moves on with its sting.

5. I don't know where literature ends and life begins,
   and I like it that way.

6. Time corrects many errors,
   yet while waiting how do you keep from making more?

7. The wound must forgive the knife.
   Nothing else can.

8. No matter what it cost or how it ended, one is always proud of a past love
   except when one is ashamed of it.

9. Santayana said, "Those who cannot remember the past are condemned to repeat it."
   But without forgetfulness, who can be optimistic?

10. Love rouses the sleeping mind—
    Cupid's kisses upon the mouth of Psyche.

11. The frog disappeared into the lily pond,
    but I loved even the brief vision.

Paraclausithyron

The ice upon the hyacinth
the black antennae of the clock
are not as cruel as the door
you shut against me.
I beg news of your dreams
the milk of your voice.
Don't waste yourself
like an unread book
hoarding your wisdom and charm
or keep yourself boxed up
like a hat too fine to get a little soiled.
Sooner or later
your joints will rust
like the hinges of this door,
everything will become harder
and harder to open.
I will wait a year, maybe two
then don't blame me if I seek
someone simpler
less in need of coaxing.

This Door or That

So that you would think of me
when you lay down and when you woke up
when you put out the cat
or brought in the mail
I gave you this gift.
Whether it was to be affixed to this door
or that, angled in or out,
touched or not, blessed or not blessed
was a matter of controversy.
But I loved the way the crafter
had lacquered some of my favorite outlaws
petals of heal-all and blue-eyed grass
onto its olive wood.
Inside it a man played guitar and a woman sang.
Suddenly one was cruel
and the other silent
for a long while. Later they ate
hot-and-sour soup
then made love so desperately
their souls flew far from life, and who knew
if they would fly back
and through which door.

Notes

Gaspara Stampa (1523–54) was an Italian Renaissance poet. She wrote hundreds of sonnets of unhappy love.

Lilith is a non-biblical figure, part ancient folk tradition, part rabbinic legend. She was said to have been Adam's wife before Eve and was created as his equal. Characterized as a self-assertive woman, Lilith refused to be subservient to Adam during sexual intercourse or in any other way and fled or was driven from Eden. She became a demon who preyed upon women in labor, caused miscarriages, and killed newborns. She also visited men in their sleep and had intercourse with them. Contemporary feminists have adopted Lilith as a symbol of rebellion and bold self-expression.

A paraclausithyron is a motif that originated in Greek and Roman poetry; it expresses a lover's lament before the beloved's closed door.

Acknowledgments

I gratefully acknowledge the following publications in which these poems, sometimes in earlier versions, first appeared:

Artful Dodge: "Eve and Lilith Go to Macy's," "Lilith at the Cosmetics Counter," and "Lilith's Quilt"

Boulevard: "Hitchhiker," "Insomniac Romance," and "Please Understand"

Bucks County Review: "The Notebook" (under the title "Gaspara Stampa's Sonnet CXXXII: An Adaptation")

Connecticut Review: "Faux King in the Parking Lot" (under the title "The Faux King")

Contemporary American Voices: "Idylls of Mayfield"

Hunger Mountain: "Action Hero"

Jewish Women's Literary Annual: "This Door or That"

kaleidowhirl: "This Life"

Kerem: "Eve and Lilith Back at the Garden" and "A Piece of Silk"

Knockout: "Miss Plastique"

Lucid Rhythms: "Vacation"

Mad Poets Review: "Dippity-do" (under the title "Vanity") and "Yes No Maybe"

Mannequin Envy: "To a Lamprey"

Nerve Cowboy: "Being Me"

The Poetry Miscellany: "Hotel Paradox"

Potomac Review: "The Grip"

Press 1: "The Language of Wildflowers"

Schuylkill Valley Journal: "The Foundations of Poetry," "People Can Get Used to Just about Anything," and "To a Rival"

Think Journal: "The House on Blackberry Lane"

Tiferet: "Twelve Lips"

U.S. 1 Worksheets: "Some First Thoughts"

Word Riot: "Eddie Pratt as Himself"

"Eve and Lilith Go to Macy's" appears in *The New Promised Land: An Anthology of Jewish American Poetry*. Deborah Ager and Matthew Silverman, eds. London, New York: Continuum.

"Idylls of Mayfield" appears in *Rabbit Ears: TV Poems*. Joel Allegretti, ed. Hoboken, NJ: Poets Wear Prada.

"Paraclausithyron" appears in *Poems for the Writing: Prompts for Poets*. Valerie Fox and Lynn Levin. Norman, OK: Texture Press.

Profound thanks to Valerie Fox and Hayden Saunier for reading an early draft of this manuscript and advising me on many of the poems. Betty Rossi, Gail Rixen, and Mary Lou Marchand of Loonfeather Press, you'll always be in my heart. Bill Donnelly, thank you for the cover and book design and for being my go-to guy. To Tony Lutkus, much gratitude for your help and advice. To Ellen Foos and Vasiliki Katsarou, my wonderful editors at Ragged Sky Press, your enthusiasm, support, gentle, and most perspicacious guidance mean the world to me. Thank you for believing in this book.

THE RAGGED SKY POETRY SERIES

Susquehanna and *The Confidence Man*
   by Michael R. Brown

The Luxury of Obstacles
   by Elizabeth Danson

Little Knitted Sister
   by Ellen Foos

Loose Parlance
   by Daniel A. Harris

Intimate Geography
   by Ishmael von Heidrick-Barnes

Moonmilk and Other Poems
   by Carlos Hernández Peña

Eating Her Wedding Dress:
A Collection of Clothing Poems
   edited by Katsarou, O'Toole, and Foos

Memento Tsunami
   by Vasiliki Katsarou

Dog Watch
   by Valerie Lawson

Miss Plastique
   by Lynn Levin

I Should Have Given Them Water
   by Eileen Malone

Between Silence and Praise
   by Elizabeth Anne Socolow

Penguins in a Warming World
   by Anca Vlasopolos

Escape Velocity
   by Arlene Weiner

LYNN LEVIN's previous collections of poems include *Fair Creatures of an Hour, Imaginarium,* and *A Few Questions about Paradise.* She is, with Valerie Fox, the author of *Poems for the Writing: Prompts for Poets.* Lynn Levin teaches at Drexel University and the University of Pennsylvania. She was born in St. Louis, Missouri and lives in Bucks County, Pennsylvania.

CPSIA information can be obtained
at www.ICGtesting.com
Printed in the USA
LVOW10s2355220117
521828LV00001B/28/P